Major Secrete Of Social Media Marketing

Preface

Welcome to The Major Secret of Social Media Marketing. In the fast-paced and ever-evolving landscape of digital communication, social media has become the linchpin of modern marketing strategies. This book is more than just a guide; it is a journey into the heart of effective social media marketing, unveiling the key principles and strategies that lie at the core of success in this dynamic realm.

The genesis of this book stems from a realization that, amidst the vast array of social media advice available, there exists a major secret—a key differentiator that separates those who merely participate from those who truly thrive. The purpose of this book is to demystify that secret and provide you with actionable insights that can elevate your social media presence to new heights.

As we delve into the chapters ahead, you will discover a comprehensive exploration of the fundamental elements that contribute to successful social media marketing campaigns. From understanding your audience to crafting compelling content, from decoding algorithms to staying ahead of platform changes, each chapter is designed to equip you with practical knowledge and strategic approaches.

Whether you are a seasoned marketing professional seeking to refine your skills or a newcomer eager to make a splash in the digital space, this book is tailored to meet you where you are. I hope that the insights within these pages will not only empower you with the knowledge to navigate the complexities of social media but will also inspire you to innovate and push the boundaries of what is possible.

The Major Secret of Social Media Marketing is more than a manual—it is a call to action. It invites you to embrace the challenges and opportunities that social media presents, encouraging you to leverage its potential to build meaningful connections, drive engagement, and propel your brand to new heights.

Thank you for embarking on this journey with me. May the pages that follow be a source of inspiration, knowledge, and transformation as you unlock the major secret of social media marketing.

— Moses Alfred

Social media manager

13 November, 2023

Foreword

In the dynamic realm of modern business, where the digital landscape constantly evolves, social media has emerged as a powerful force reshaping the way we connect, communicate, and conduct commerce. The Major Secret of Social Media Marketing is a compelling exploration into the depths of this transformative tool, unveiling the strategies and insights that distinguish success from mere participation.

As we navigate an era inundated with information and connectivity, the need for businesses to harness the potential of social media has never been more critical. In this book, the author unravels the enigma surrounding effective social media marketing, offering a roadmap that transcends conventional approaches. With astute observations, practical tips, and a keen understanding of the ever-changing social media landscape, The Major Secret of Social Media Marketing equips readers with the knowledge to not only navigate this intricate terrain but thrive in it.

The author, drawing from a wealth of experience and research, delves into the nuances of audience engagement, content creation, and the subtle art of building a brand in the digital age. From decoding algorithms to mastering the psychology of social media users, this book is a comprehensive guide that empowers marketers, entrepreneurs, and enthusiasts alike to leverage the full potential of social platforms.

What sets this book apart is its commitment to demystifying the complexities of social media marketing, making it accessible to beginners while providing seasoned professionals with fresh perspectives. The Major Secret of Social Media Marketing is not just a guide; it is a companion for those navigating the ever-evolving landscape of online influence and brand building.

In an age where digital presence is synonymous with relevance, understanding the major secret is not just an advantage but a necessity. As you embark on this insightful journey through the pages of this book, prepare to unlock the doors to a world where social media becomes not just a tool but a strategic ally in your quest for business success.

— Gospel Gwrite
  Meta ad expert/Business developer
  12 October, 2023

Acknowledgment

I would like to express my sincere gratitude to all those who have contributed to the creation of this book on social media marketing. Special thanks to my dedicated team for their unwavering support and collaborative efforts throughout the writing process. I also extend my appreciation to the professionals and experts in the field whose insights have enriched the content of this book. Lastly, heartfelt thanks to my family and friends for their encouragement and understanding during this undertaking. This book is a culmination of collective expertise and shared enthusiasm for the dynamic world of social media marketing.

Table of Contents:

CHAPTER 1

INTRODUCTION

POWER OF SOCIAL MEDIA MARKETING:
Social media marketing is a powerful and influential tool for businesses and individuals in today's digital age. It has transformed the way companies connect with their audience, build brand awareness, and drive sales.

While the power of social media marketing is undeniable, it's important to approach it strategically. A well-thought-out social media marketing plan tailored to your business goals and audience is essential for success. Additionally, the landscape is constantly evolving, so staying up-to-date with the latest trends and platform changes is crucial to maintaining a strong online presence.

UNLOCKING SECRETS: Unlocking secrets can have varying significance depending on the context. It can deepen knowledge, aid problem-solving, promote justice and accountability, facilitate healing and closure, foster healthy relationships, spur personal growth, enhance national security, drive innovation, preserve cultural heritage, and ensure transparency. However, ethical considerations, privacy, and security must be carefully weighed when seeking to uncover secrets. Approach with caution and awareness of potential consequences.

CHAPTER 2

Content creation and strategy

Content creation and strategy are integral components of digital marketing and communication efforts for businesses and individuals. These activities involve the development and planning of content to achieve specific goals. Here's an overview of content creation and strategy:

Content Creation:
1. **Content Types:** Content can take various forms, such as blog posts, articles, videos, infographics, podcasts, social media updates, and more. The choice of content type depends on the target audience and the message you want to convey.
2. **Quality and Relevance**: Creating high-quality and relevant content is essential. It should provide value to the audience, whether through information, entertainment, or solving a problem.
3. **Consistency**: Consistent content creation helps build an audience and maintain their

interest. Regular posting schedules can keep your audience engaged.

4. Visual and Aesthetic Elements: Visual content is increasingly important. Including appealing images, videos, and graphics can enhance the appeal of your content.

5. Keyword Optimization: For online content, incorporating relevant keywords helps improve visibility in search engines (SEO). However, it's important to avoid keyword stuffing and ensure that content reads naturally.

6. Originality: Original content is valued by both audiences and search engines. Plagiarism should be avoided, and proper citations given when necessary.

7. Storytelling: Effective content often involves storytelling. Narratives can make information more engaging and relatable.

Content Strategy:

1. Audience Research: Understanding your target audience's needs, interests, and preferences is the foundation of content strategy. This knowledge informs the type of content to create.

2. Goal Setting: Define clear objectives for your content, such as increasing brand awareness, driving website traffic, generating leads, or boosting sales.

3. Content Calendar: A content calendar helps plan and schedule content creation and publication. It ensures a consistent flow of content.

4. Distribution Channels: Determine which platforms and channels are most suitable for your audience. Social media, email, blogs, and video-sharing sites are common distribution channels.

5. Engagement and Interaction: Encourage audience engagement through comments, likes, shares, and responses. Interaction with the audience can build relationships and trust.

6. Monitoring and Analysis: Regularly assess the performance of your content using analytics tools. This data helps refine your strategy by identifying what works and what needs improvement.

7. Adaptation: Be flexible and ready to adapt your content strategy as needed. Market trends, audience preferences, and technology can change rapidly.

8. Promotion and SEO: Promote your content through various means, including social media, email marketing, and paid advertising. Effective use of SEO techniques can improve your content's visibility.

9. Consistency with Brand Identity: Ensure that your content aligns with your brand's identity, values, and messaging.

10. Measuring ROI: Evaluate the return on investment of your content strategy. Determine whether it's achieving its intended goals and adjust as necessary.

Crafting engaging content

Crafting engaging content is essential for capturing and maintaining your audience's attention, whether you're creating blog posts, social media updates, videos, or any other type of content. Here are some key strategies to help you create content that keeps your audience engaged:

1. Know Your Audience: Understand your target audience's preferences, interests, and needs. Tailor your content to resonate with them.

2. Compelling Headlines: Craft attention-grabbing headlines that pique curiosity and encourage people to click or read further.

3. Clear and Concise Writing: Write clearly and straightforwardly. Avoid jargon and long, convoluted sentences. Make your content easy to understand.

4. Tell a Story: Storytelling is a powerful way to engage your audience. Use anecdotes, narratives, and personal experiences to connect with readers or viewers.

5. Visual Appeal: Incorporate images, videos, infographics, and other visual elements to break up text and make your content more visually appealing.

6. Use Bullet Points and Lists: Break down complex information into easily digestible, scannable lists or bullet points. This makes your content more reader-friendly.

7. Keep it Relevant: Ensure your content is relevant to your target audience and aligns with their interests and needs.

8. Unique and Valuable Content: Offer unique insights, perspectives, or information that can't be easily found elsewhere. Providing value to your audience is key.

9. Use Conversational Tone: Write in a conversational style that feels approachable and relatable. Avoid overly formal or academic language, unless your audience expects it.

10. Embrace Emotion: Create content that elicits emotional responses. Whether it's humor, empathy, excitement, or inspiration, emotions can deeply engage your audience.

11. Interactive Elements: Encourage audience interaction through comments, questions, polls, and calls to action. Make them feel involved in the conversation.

12. Consistency: Maintain a consistent posting schedule so your audience knows when to expect new content. Regularity can help build a dedicated following.

13. Variety: Mix up the types of content you create. Use a combination of articles, videos, podcasts, and other formats to cater to different preferences.

14. Solve Problems: Address common challenges or questions your audience faces. Providing solutions or guidance can make your content highly valuable.

15. Engage with Your Audience: Respond to comments and engage in conversations with your audience. This fosters a sense of community and connection.

16. Call to Action (CTA): Include a clear CTA at the end of your content, guiding your audience on what to do next, whether it's subscribing, sharing, or making a purchase.

17. Optimize for Mobile: Ensure that your content is mobile-friendly, as many people access content on smartphones and tablets.

18. A/B Testing: Experiment with different content strategies and formats, and analyze which ones resonate best with your audience through A/B testing.

19. Feedback and Iteration: Pay attention to feedback and analytics to refine your content over time. Adapt to changing audience preferences and trends.

20. Creativity and Uniqueness: Be creative and strive for uniqueness. Stand out by offering a fresh perspective, style, or approach that sets your content apart.

Remember that crafting engaging content is an ongoing process. Stay attuned to your audience's feedback and evolving interests, and be willing to adapt and experiment to keep your content engaging and relevant.

Content planning and scheduling

Content planning and scheduling are critical aspects of an effective content marketing strategy. They help you maintain consistency, save time, and ensure your content aligns with your goals and audience. Here's how to plan and schedule your content effectively:

1. Define Your Content Goals: - Start by clarifying your content marketing objectives. Do you aim to increase brand awareness, generate leads, boost website traffic, or provide value to your audience?

2. Understand Your Audience:
   - Research your target audience's preferences, needs, and behaviors. What content formats do they prefer? What topics interest them?

3. Develop a Content Calendar: - Create a content calendar that outlines when and what type of content you'll publish. Consider using tools like content management systems (CMS), editorial calendars, or digital marketing platforms for scheduling.

4. Content Ideas and Topics:
   - Brainstorm a list of content ideas and topics that align with your objectives and audience.

These can include blog posts, videos, infographics, webinars, and more.

5. Content Formats: - Decide on the content formats you'll use. Mixing formats, such as written content, images, videos, podcasts, and social media updates, can cater to a broader audience.

6. Keyword Research: - If your content is web-based, conduct keyword research to identify relevant keywords and phrases that can improve your content's search engine visibility.

7. Assign Responsibilities: - Determine who will create, edit, and review the content. Clearly define roles and responsibilities to ensure a smooth content production process.

8. Content Creation: - Develop your content based on the topics and formats you've chosen. Maintain a consistent and high-quality output.

9. Scheduling: - Use content scheduling tools or platforms to plan and set publication dates for your content. This allows you to post at the most effective times for your audience.

10. Social Media Promotion: - If your content is shared on social media, schedule posts to promote it at optimal times. Consider using social media management tools to automate posting.

11. Consistency: - Stick to your content calendar and be consistent with your posting schedule. Regularity helps build an audience and fosters anticipation.

12. Monitoring and Analysis: - Track the performance of your content. Use analytics tools to measure metrics like engagement, click-through rates, and conversions. This data informs future content decisions.

13. Adjust and Refine: - Based on the analysis, adjust your content strategy. You may need to refine your topics, formats, or posting times to better resonate with your audience.

14. Evergreen and Timely Content: - Balance your content mix with evergreen content (timeless) and timely content (related to current events or trends)

15. Repurposing: - Consider repurposing existing content into different formats or updating older content to keep it relevant and valuable.

16. Stay Organized: - Maintain a well-organized content repository, ensuring easy access to past content for future reference and repurposing.

17. Content Promotion: - Don't forget to promote your content beyond your platforms. Reach out to influencers, collaborate with partners, and use email marketing to extend your content's reach. Effective content planning and scheduling help streamline your content marketing efforts and ensure that your content aligns with your goals and resonates with your audience. Regular assessment and adaptation based on performance data are key to long-term success.

Chapter 3

Audience Analysis and Targeting

Audience analysis and targeting are fundamental steps in creating a successful marketing strategy. Understanding your audience allows you to tailor your messaging, content, and campaigns to effectively reach and engage the right people. Here's how to conduct audience analysis and targeting:

Audience Analysis:
1. **Demographics:** Gather information about your audience's age, gender, location, education level, income, and other demographic factors. This data helps you create a basic profile of your typical customer.
2. **Psychographics:** Explore your audience's values, beliefs, interests, and lifestyles. This information provides insights into their motivations and preferences.

3. Behavior: Analyze the behaviors of your audience. Consider their online and offline activities, shopping habits, and product usage. It helps in understanding how they interact with your brand.

4. Needs and Pain Points: Identify the needs, challenges, and pain points of your audience. This understanding helps you tailor your messaging to address their specific concerns.

5. Purchase Journey: Map out your audience's purchase journey from awareness to consideration and conversion. Recognize touchpoints and key decision-making moments.

6. Competitive Analysis: Study your competitors' audiences. What demographics, psychographics, and behaviors are they targeting, and how can you differentiate your approach?

7. Surveys and Feedback: Collect feedback through surveys and social media interactions to gain direct insights into what your audience thinks and wants.

8. Data Analytics: Use web analytics and social media insights to monitor audience behavior on your digital platforms. These tools can provide detailed information about your audience's online activities.

Audience Targeting:

1. Segmentation: Divide your audience into distinct segments based on shared characteristics, needs, or behaviors. This segmentation allows you to craft tailored messages for each group.

2. Buyer Personas: Develop detailed buyer personas for different audience segments. A buyer persona is a semi-fictional representation of your ideal customer, encompassing demographics, behaviors, and goals.

3. Content Personalization: Customize your content and messaging to speak directly to each audience segment. Personalization can significantly increase engagement.

4. Ad Campaigns: When running advertising campaigns, use audience targeting features on platforms like Google Ads and Facebook Ads to reach specific groups that match your ideal customer profile.

5. Email Marketing: Segment your email list to send targeted messages to subscribers based on their preferences, behaviors, or past interactions with your brand.

6. Geographic Targeting: If your business serves specific locations, use geotargeting to reach audiences in those areas.

7. Social Media Targeting: Utilize social media advertising to narrow down your audience based on demographics, interests, and behaviors.

8. Remarketing: Retarget website visitors or past customers with customized ads to re-engage and encourage them to complete desired actions.

9. A/B Testing: Experiment with different targeting approaches and assess which strategies are most effective in reaching and converting your target audience.

10. Regular Review and Optimization: Continuously monitor the performance of your targeting efforts and adjust your strategy as needed based on the results.

Effective audience analysis and targeting enable you to create more relevant and compelling content and marketing campaigns, which, in turn, lead to better engagement, conversions, and customer satisfaction. It's an ongoing process that requires adaptation as your audience evolves and as market conditions change.

Understanding your audience

Understanding your audience is a fundamental aspect of effective communication, marketing, and content creation. By gaining insights into your audience, you can tailor your messaging and content to better resonate with their needs and preferences. Here's how to understand your audience:

1. Market Research: - Start by conducting market research to gather demographic and psychographic data about your audience. This includes information like age, gender, location, income, interests, values, and behaviors.

2. Surveys and Questionnaires: - Create surveys or questionnaires to collect specific data from your audience. Ask about their preferences, challenges, and expectations.

3. Analytics and Data: - Use web analytics and social media insights to understand your audience's online behavior. These tools provide valuable information about their interactions with your digital platforms.

4. Competitive Analysis: - Study your competitors' audiences. What demographics, behaviors, and preferences are they targeting? This can help you differentiate your approach.

5. Customer Feedback: - Collect feedback from your existing customers through reviews, feedback forms, and customer service interactions. Pay attention to both positive and negative feedback to identify areas for improvement.

6. Buyer Personas: - Develop detailed buyer personas, which are semi-fictional representations of your ideal customers. These personas should encompass demographic and psychographic details, behaviors, and goals.

7. Social Listening: - Monitor social media conversations related to your industry or brand. This can provide insights into trends, sentiment, and what matters to your audience.

8. Focus Groups: - Organize focus groups or interviews with a small sample of your target audience to gain qualitative insights. This approach allows for in-depth understanding and direct feedback.

9. Feedback and Surveys: - Encourage direct communication with your audience through feedback forms, comment sections, and social media interactions. Respond to questions and comments to build trust.

10. Review Customer Data: - Analyze transaction histories, customer behavior, and other relevant data to understand purchasing patterns and preferences.

11. Testing and Experimentation: - Test different messaging, content formats, and marketing approaches to see what resonates most with your audience. A/B testing can be a valuable tool for this purpose.

12. Adapt and Evolve: - Audience understanding is an ongoing process. Regularly update your knowledge and adapt your strategies as your audience evolves and as market conditions change.

The more you understand your audience, the better you can cater to their needs, deliver relevant content, and build lasting relationships. This understanding helps you create more effective marketing campaigns, product offerings, and content that genuinely connects with your target demographic.

Effective targeting strategies

Effective targeting strategies are crucial for reaching the right audience with your marketing efforts. By focusing on the most receptive and relevant individuals or groups, you can maximize the impact of your campaigns and improve conversion rates. Here are some effective targeting strategies:

1. Demographic Targeting: - Segment your audience based on demographic factors such as age, gender, income, education, marital status, and occupation. This helps tailor your messaging to specific groups.

2. Geographic Targeting:- Narrow your audience based on location, such as country, state, city, or even zip code. This is especially important for local businesses or those with location-specific offers.

3. Psychographic Targeting: - Consider the psychological aspects of your audience, including their interests, values, lifestyle, and personality traits. This approach helps you connect with people on a deeper level.

4. Behavioral Targeting: - Analyze user behavior, such as online browsing habits, previous purchases, and interactions with your website or app. Tailor your content and offers based on these actions.

5. Contextual Targeting: - Place ads or content in contextually relevant environments. For example, display your gardening product ads on websites or content related to gardening.

6. Remarketing/Retargeting:- Target users who have previously interacted with your website or app but didn't convert. Remarketing allows you to re-engage them with tailored content or offers.

7. Lookalike Audiences:- Create audiences that resemble your existing customers. Platforms like Facebook and Google Ads offer lookalike audience features to reach users with similar characteristics and behaviors.

8. Device and Platform Targeting: - Choose which devices (desktop, mobile, tablet) and platforms (iOS, Android) to target based on where your audience is most active.

9. Email List Segmentation: - Segment your email list to send targeted messages to subscribers based on their preferences, behaviors, or past interactions with your brand.

10. Time and Dayparting: - Determine the most effective times and days to target your audience. Schedule your content or ads to coincide with when your audience is most active.

11. Interests and Hobbies: - Consider what hobbies and interests your audience has and target your content or products accordingly. For example, if you sell sporting equipment, target users interested in sports.

12. B2B Targeting: - For business-to-business marketing, target specific industries, job titles, company sizes, or even specific companies to reach decision-makers and influencers.

13. Influencer Marketing:- Collaborate with influencers who have a following that matches your target audience. Their endorsement can help you reach a more engaged and relevant audience.

14. Affinity Audiences: - Use Google Ads' affinity audiences to target users who have demonstrated a strong interest in specific topics or industries related to your products or services.

15. Loyalty and Customer Segmentation: - Create campaigns specifically for your loyal customers or high-value clients. Reward their loyalty with exclusive offers and personalized content.

16. A/B Testing: - Continuously test different targeting strategies to determine which ones are the most effective in reaching and converting your target audience.

Effective targeting strategies can significantly enhance the efficiency of your marketing efforts, reduce ad spend wastage, and boost your return on investment. Regularly review and adjust your targeting methods to stay aligned with evolving audience behaviors and market trends

Chapter 4

Building a strong online presence

Building a strong online presence is crucial for individuals and businesses alike. It helps establish credibility, reach a wider audience, and achieve various personal or professional goals. Here's a step-by-step guide to building a strong online presence:

1. Define Your Goals: - Determine your objectives for your online presence. Do you want to increase brand awareness, generate leads, sell products, share expertise, or connect with a specific community? Clearly defined goals will guide your strategy.

2. Identify Your Target Audience: - Understand your ideal audience's demographics, interests, and needs. Tailoring your online presence to their preferences is essential for success.

3. Create High-Quality Content: - Develop valuable, relevant, and engaging content that speaks to your target audience. This can include blog posts, videos, social media updates, podcasts, and more.

4. Optimize for Search Engines (SEO): - Implement SEO best practices to ensure your content is discoverable by search engines. This includes keyword research, optimizing meta tags, and improving website speed and mobile-friendliness.

5. Choose the Right Platforms: - Select the online platforms that align with your goals and where your target audience is most active. This may include websites, social media, forums, or email marketing.

6. Consistency is Key: - Maintain a consistent posting schedule to keep your audience engaged and build trust. Regularly encourages return visits.

7. Engage with Your Audience: - Interact with your audience through comments, direct messages, and social media conversations. Respond to questions and feedback promptly.

8. Leverage Social Media: - Use social media platforms to share content, engage with followers, and promote your brand. Each platform has its unique strengths, so tailor your approach accordingly.

9. Build an Email List: - Collect email addresses from interested visitors to build a direct line of communication. Use email marketing to share updates and offers.

10. Networking and Collaborations: - Connect with individuals and businesses in your niche or industry. Collaborations, partnerships, and guest posting can help expand your reach.

11. Personal Branding: - Invest in your brand by showcasing your expertise, values, and personality. This humanizes your online presence and builds authenticity.

12. Online Reputation Management: - Monitor and manage your online reputation. Respond to reviews and address any negative feedback professionally.

13. Measurement and Analytics: - Use analytics tools to track the performance of your online presence. Monitor website traffic, engagement metrics, and conversion rates, and adjust your strategy accordingly.

14. Paid Advertising: - Consider paid advertising on platforms like Google Ads or social media to reach a wider audience or promote specific content or products.

15. Adapt to Trends: - Stay updated on industry trends, algorithm changes, and emerging technologies. Adapt your strategy to incorporate new opportunities and best practices.

16. Website Optimization: - Ensure your website is user-friendly, loads quickly, and provides a seamless experience for visitors. Mobile optimization is crucial.

17. Community Building: - Foster an online community around your brand or interests. Encourage discussions, user-generated content, and engagement among your audience.

Building a strong online presence takes time, effort, and consistency. It's an ongoing process that involves regular assessment and adaptation to meet the changing needs and preferences of your audience and the digital landscape.

Branding and consistency

Branding and consistency go hand in hand and are crucial elements for establishing a strong and recognizable identity for individuals and businesses. Here's why branding and consistency are essential:

1. Branding Defines Your Identity: - Branding encompasses your values, mission, vision, and the overall image you want to project. It sets the foundation for how you want to be perceived by your audience.

2. Recognition and Trust: - A consistent brand identity helps in creating recognition. When your audience sees your logo, colors, or messaging consistently across various touchpoints, it fosters trust and familiarity.

3. Message Clarity: - A well-defined brand with consistent messaging ensures that your audience clearly understands what you offer, your unique value proposition, and what you stand for.

4. Differentiation: - Effective branding sets you apart from your competitors. It helps you define what makes your business or personal brand unique and valuable.

5. Content Cohesion: - Consistency in branding extends to the content you create and share. Whether it's blog posts, social media updates, videos, or advertising, a cohesive brand identity makes your content more impactful.

6. Professionalism: - A consistent brand image reflects professionalism and reliability. It conveys that you pay attention to details and care about your audience's experience.

7. Loyalty and Advocacy: - A strong brand identity can foster customer loyalty and advocacy. People are more likely to become repeat customers and recommend your brand to others when they have a positive and consistent experience.

8. Easy Decision-Making: - Consistency simplifies decision-making for your audience. When your brand consistently delivers quality and reliability, your audience can trust that they'll receive the same experience each time.

9. Cross-Platform Recognition: - In an era of multi-channel marketing, consistency helps maintain a seamless brand experience across various platforms, including websites, social media, print materials, and in-person interactions.

10. Adaptability and Evolution:- While consistency is vital, it doesn't mean your brand can't evolve. You can adapt your branding to changing market trends or audience needs while maintaining core elements that define your identity.

11. Employee Alignment: - A strong brand with consistent values and messaging helps align employees with the organization's mission and goals. This internal consistency translates to external consistency.

12. Long-Term Success: - Consistency in branding contributes to long-term success. It builds a solid foundation for growth and expansion while maintaining the trust of your audience.

To maintain brand consistency, you should:

- Develop brand guidelines that outline key elements like logo usage, color schemes, typography, tone of voice, and messaging principles.
- Train employees and collaborators on your brand guidelines to ensure consistent application.
- Regularly review and update your branding to stay relevant and align with your evolving goals.
- Monitor and measure the effectiveness of your branding efforts to identify areas for improvement.

Remember that branding and consistency are not one-time efforts; they are ongoing commitments that require attention and care to ensure your brand remains strong and relevant in the eyes of your audience.

Leveraging multiple platforms

Leveraging multiple platforms in your marketing and advertising strategy can be highly beneficial for reaching a broader audience and maximizing your campaign's impact. Here are some key points to consider when utilizing multiple platforms:

1. Diversify Your Reach: Each platform has its unique user base and features. By using multiple platforms, you can reach a more diverse and varied audience. For example, some platforms may be better for targeting younger demographics, while others might be more effective for reaching professionals.

2. Multichannel Consistency: While you're using different platforms, maintain consistency in your branding, messaging, and overall marketing strategy. This ensures a cohesive and recognizable brand presence across all channels.

3. Adapt Content: Tailor your content to each platform's specific audience and format. What works on Facebook may not work on Twitter or Instagram. Create content that resonates with the expectations and behaviors of users on each platform.

4. Cross-Promotion: Cross-promote your content and campaigns across platforms. For example, if you're running a promotion on Instagram, share it on Facebook and Twitter. This extends the reach of your campaign and encourages your existing audience to engage on other platforms.

5. Analytics and Insights: Use the analytics and insights provided by each platform to understand what's working and what's not. Adjust your strategy based on data-driven insights to optimize your campaigns.

6. Timing and Scheduling: Different platforms have different peak usage times. Be mindful of when your target audience is most active on each platform and schedule your posts or ads accordingly.

7. Paid Advertising: Consider using paid advertising on multiple platforms to boost your reach. Platforms like Facebook Ads, Google Ads, and Instagram Ads offer highly targeted options for reaching your ideal audience.

8. Customer Journey Mapping: Understand your customer's journey and how they interact with your brand across different platforms. This knowledge can help you create a more personalized and effective marketing strategy.

9. Stay Updated: Social media and advertising platforms are constantly evolving. Stay updated with the latest trends and changes in algorithms to ensure your strategies remain effective.

10. A/B Testing: Use A/B testing to determine which platforms and content strategies deliver the best results. Experiment with different approaches and measure the outcomes to fine-tune your campaigns.

11. Budget Allocation: Allocate your budget wisely across platforms based on the performance and goals of each. Some platforms may require a higher budget, while others may deliver better results with a more modest investment.

12. Monitor Competitors: Keep an eye on what your competitors are doing across various platforms. Analyze their strategies and adapt where necessary to stay competitive.

Leveraging multiple platforms can be a powerful way to connect with your target audience and drive your marketing and advertising efforts.

However, it's essential to approach it strategically, with a clear understanding of each platform's

Chapter 5

Community engagement

Community engagement is a multifaceted concept that involves actively involving and interacting with a specific group or community, whether it's an online community, a local neighborhood, a customer base, or any other defined group of people. It's a way to build relationships, share information, and collaborate with the community for mutual benefit. Here are some key aspects of community engagement:

1. Listening and Understanding: Effective community engagement starts with active listening. Understand the needs, concerns, and aspirations of the community. Conduct surveys, interviews, or social listening to gather insights.

2. Two-Way Communication: It's not just about broadcasting information but fostering a two-way conversation. Encourage feedback, questions, and discussions. Respond to comments and messages promptly.

3. Transparency: Be open and transparent in your communications. Share information, both positive and negative, and be honest about your intentions and actions.

4. Value Addition: Provide value to the community. Offer information, resources, or solutions that address their interests or issues. This can be in the form of content, services, or events.

5. Build Trust: Trust is a cornerstone of community engagement. Consistency, reliability, and genuine care for the community's well-being are essential for building trust.

6. Empowerment: Encourage community members to take ownership and contribute. Give them the tools and resources to make a difference in their community.

7. Accessibility: Ensure that community engagement efforts are accessible to all, regardless of their background, abilities, or demographics. Use inclusive language and accessible formats for information.

8. Online and Offline Engagement: Depending on your community, engagement can take place both online and offline. Utilize social media, websites, forums, and physical events to reach your audience.

9. Customization: Recognize that different communities may have different preferences and needs. Tailor your engagement strategies to suit the specific community you're targeting.

10. Consistency: Regular and ongoing engagement is crucial. Don't engage with the community only when you need something; make it a continuous effort.

11. Collaboration: Seek opportunities to collaborate with the community on projects, initiatives, or events. Collaborative efforts can strengthen the sense of belonging and shared goals.

12. Measuring Impact: Establish metrics and key performance indicators to measure the impact of your community engagement efforts. Track engagement levels, feedback, and the outcomes of your initiatives.

13. Feedback Loop: Use feedback from the community to improve your products, services, or community engagement strategies. Show that their input is valued and acted upon.

14. Conflict Resolution: Address conflicts and disagreements within the community fairly and respectfully. Establish guidelines for handling disputes or issues.

15. Celebrating Successes: Recognize and celebrate the achievements and contributions of community members. This encourages further engagement and creates a positive atmosphere. Community engagement is not a one-size-fits-all approach. It requires adaptability, empathy, and a genuine commitment to nurturing relationships with the community. Successful community engagement can lead to a more loyal customer base, improved social cohesion, and a better understanding of your audience's needs and expectations.

Fostering meaningful connections

Fostering meaningful connections, whether in personal relationships or professional contexts, is essential for building trust, creating positive experiences, and nurturing strong bonds. Here are some key principles and strategies to help you foster such connections:

1. Active Listening: One of the most crucial aspects of building meaningful connections is being an active and empathetic listener. Pay close attention to what the other person is saying, show genuine interest, and ask open-ended questions to encourage them to share more.

2. Authenticity: Be yourself in your interactions. Authenticity helps people feel comfortable and allows them to connect with the real you. Pretending to be someone you're not can lead to superficial connections.

3. Empathy: Put yourself in the other person's shoes. Try to understand their feelings, perspectives, and needs. Empathy shows that you care about their well-being.

4. Respect: Respect is the foundation of any meaningful connection. Treat others with kindness, courtesy, and consideration. Respect their boundaries and beliefs, even if they differ from your own.

5. Vulnerability: Sharing your thoughts, feelings, and experiences, including your vulnerabilities, can create a deeper connection. It can help others relate to you on a more personal level.

6. Shared Interests and Values: Find common interests and values that you can bond over. Shared hobbies, passions, or beliefs can create a strong sense of connection.

7. Quality Time: Dedicate quality time to your interactions. Put away distractions, be present in the moment, and give your full attention to the person you're connecting with.

8. Supportive Communication: Offer support and encouragement when needed. Be a source of inspiration and motivation for others in their pursuits and challenges.

9. Gratitude: Express gratitude for the people in your life. Recognize and appreciate their contributions and the positive impact they have on you.

10. Consistency: Building meaningful connections often requires consistent effort. Regularly check in with people, celebrate milestones together, and stay connected over time.

11. Reciprocity: Be willing to give as well as receive. Meaningful connections are a two-way street, and both parties should contribute to the relationship.

12. Boundaries: While connections are important, it's also essential to respect boundaries. Everyone needs personal space and time, and it's crucial to recognize and honor these boundaries.

13. Conflict Resolution: Conflicts can arise in any relationship. When they do, address them openly and constructively. Finding solutions and compromises can lead to stronger connections.

14. Acts of Kindness: Small acts of kindness, whether through compliments, favors, or gestures, can go a long way in building connections and making others feel valued.

15. Forgiveness: Be open to forgiving and moving past mistakes or conflicts. Holding onto grudges can hinder the growth of meaningful connections.

16. Networking: In professional contexts, networking plays a significant role in fostering meaningful connections. Attend industry events, join professional organizations, and seek out opportunities to connect with like-minded individuals.

Fostering meaningful connections takes time, effort, and sincerity. Whether in personal or professional settings, these connections can enrich your life, provide support in times of need, and lead to fulfilling relationships that stand the test of time.

The art of responding and interacting

The art of responding and interacting effectively is crucial in various aspects of life, from personal relationships to business communication. Here are some principles to keep in mind when mastering this art:

1. Active Listening: Actively listen to the other person. This means giving them your full attention, avoiding interrupting, and showing genuine interest in what they have to say. Make eye contact, nod, and use verbal cues like "I see" or "Tell me more" to show you're engaged.

2. Empathy: Put yourself in the other person's shoes and try to understand their perspective, feelings, and needs. Empathy helps you connect on a deeper level and respond more effectively.

3. Ask Open-Ended Questions: Encourage conversation by asking open-ended questions that require more than a simple yes or no answer. This allows the other person to share their thoughts and feelings more freely.

4. Clarify and Paraphrase: To ensure you've understood the other person correctly, paraphrase what they've said and ask for clarification if needed. This demonstrates that you value their input.

5. Non-Verbal Communication: Be mindful of your non-verbal cues, such as facial expressions, body language, and tone of voice. These play a significant role in how your responses are perceived.

6. Respect and Courtesy: Maintain a respectful and courteous tone in your interactions. Treat others as you would like to be treated, even in challenging situations.

7. Constructive Feedback: When providing feedback or responding to criticism, focus on constructive and specific points. Avoid personal attacks and focus on the issue at hand.

8. Stay Calm: In emotionally charged interactions, remain composed and avoid reacting impulsively. Take a moment to collect your thoughts before responding.

9. Be Patient: Some conversations may require time and multiple interactions to resolve. Be patient and persistent when necessary.

10. Offer Solutions: When addressing problems or concerns, focus on finding solutions rather than dwelling on the issues. Collaborate with the other person to come up with mutually beneficial solutions.

11. Adapt to Communication Styles: People have different communication styles and preferences. Adapt your approach to match the other person's style for more effective interaction.

12. Acknowledge and Appreciate: Express gratitude and acknowledgment when someone shares their thoughts, helps, or contributes in any way. A simple "thank you" can go a long way.

13. Maintain Boundaries: In professional settings, it's essential to maintain appropriate boundaries and respect privacy. Don't pry into personal matters without permission.

14. Online Communication: Be mindful of your online interactions, including emails, social media, and messaging apps. Tone and intent can be easily misinterpreted, so choose your words carefully.

15. Follow-Up: After a conversation or interaction, follow up as needed. This shows you're committed to the ongoing relationship or issue.

16. Learn and Improve: Reflect on your interactions, both positive and negative, to continually improve your communication skills. Consider what worked and what could have been done better.

The art of responding and interacting is a valuable skill that can improve relationships, resolve conflicts, and enhance communication. By practicing these principles, you can become a more effective and empathetic communicator.

Chapter 6

Data analytics and performance tracking

Data analytics and performance tracking are essential components of decision-making and optimization in various fields, including business, marketing, finance, healthcare, and more. They involve collecting, analyzing, and interpreting data to gain insights, make informed decisions, and measure the success of strategies or initiatives. Here are key aspects of data analytics and performance tracking:

1. **Data Collection:** Gathering relevant data is the initial step. This can include information from various sources, such as customer databases, website interactions, social media, surveys, and more.

2. **Data Quality:** Ensure data accuracy, consistency, and completeness. Clean and high-quality data is crucial for reliable analysis and tracking.

3. **Data Storage:** Organize and store data in a structured manner, often using databases or data warehouses. Cloud-based solutions are commonly used for scalability and accessibility.

4. **Data Cleaning and Preprocessing:** Prepare data for analysis by cleaning, transforming, and

standardizing it. This step helps remove inconsistencies and outliers.

5. Data Analysis: Employ statistical, machine learning, or other analytical techniques to uncover patterns, trends, and relationships within the data.

6. Visualization: Present data in a visually understandable way using charts, graphs, dashboards, and other visual aids. Visualization can make complex data more comprehensible.

7. Key Performance Indicators (KPIs): Define KPIs that align with your goals and objectives. These metrics provide a clear measure of performance and success.

8. Benchmarking: Compare your performance data against industry benchmarks or competitors to gain insights into how well you are doing relative to your peers.

9. Predictive Analytics: Use historical data to make predictions about future outcomes. Machine learning models, regression analysis, and time series forecasting can be helpful.

10. Continuous Monitoring: Track performance regularly, not just as a one-time effort. Continuous monitoring allows you to detect trends and respond to changes in real time.

11. A/B Testing: In marketing and product development, A/B testing is commonly used to compare the effectiveness of two versions of a product or campaign to determine which performs better.

12. ROI Analysis: Calculate the return on investment (ROI) for various initiatives. This helps you understand the cost-effectiveness of your actions.

13. Data Privacy and Security: Ensure that data is handled and stored securely, particularly when dealing with sensitive or personal information.

14. Data Interpretation: Translate data insights into actionable strategies and decisions. Effective interpretation is vital for turning data into valuable knowledge.

15. Data-Driven Decision-Making: Use data to inform decision-making processes. Data-driven decisions are often more accurate and objective than those based on intuition alone.

16. Feedback Loops: Create feedback loops to implement changes and improvements based on data insights. This ensures that you adapt and optimize over time.

17. Data Reporting: Develop regular reports or dashboards that summarize key findings and performance metrics for various stakeholders.

18. Communication: Share data insights and findings with relevant team members and decision-makers to ensure alignment and collaboration.

19. Training and Education: Provide training and resources for employees to improve data literacy and the ability to work with data effectively.

20. Adaptation: Be flexible in adapting your strategies based on changing data and circumstances. Continuous improvement is key to long-term success.

Data analytics and performance tracking empower organizations to make informed decisions, identify areas for improvement, and maximize their efficiency and effectiveness. In today's data-driven world, these practices are essential for staying competitive and achieving success.

The Role of Data in Decision-Making

Data plays a central and increasingly pivotal role in decision-making across various domains, from business and healthcare to government and academia. Here are the key aspects of the role of data in decision-making:

1. Informed Decision-Making: Data provides valuable information and insights that allow decision-makers to be well informed. It supports the decision-making process by offering a factual basis for choices.

2. Objective Analysis: Data-based decisions tend to be more objective and less subject to bias or personal opinions. They rely on empirical evidence rather than intuition or anecdotal evidence.

3. Risk Management: Data helps in assessing and mitigating risks. By analyzing historical data and predicting future trends, decision-makers can make informed choices to manage and reduce risks effectively.

4. Performance Evaluation: Organizations use data to evaluate the performance of various processes, projects, and initiatives. It aids in understanding what's working well and what needs improvement.

5. Resource Allocation: Data helps allocate resources efficiently. Organizations can determine where to invest time, money, and manpower based on the data's insights into areas with the most potential for success.

6. Customer Insights: In business, data on customer behavior, preferences, and feedback are invaluable for tailoring products, services, and marketing strategies to meet customer needs.

7. Competitive Advantage: Data analysis can uncover opportunities for gaining a competitive advantage. Understanding market trends, customer behavior, and competitor strategies helps organizations stay ahead.

8. Scientific Research: In academia and scientific research, data is fundamental for hypothesis testing, experimentation, and drawing meaningful conclusions.

9. Healthcare Decision-Making: Medical professionals rely on patient data and medical research to make diagnoses, treatment plans, and health-related decisions.

10. Policy and Governance: Governments use data to develop policies, allocate resources, and measure the effectiveness of public programs and initiatives.

11. Environmental Planning: Environmental data informs decisions related to conservation, climate change, resource management, and sustainability efforts.

12. Personal Decision-Making: Even in personal life, individuals use data when making decisions, such as choosing a place to live, making investment decisions, or selecting a school for their children.

13. Real-Time Decision-Making: Data is used for real-time decision-making, especially in fields like finance, logistics, and emergency response. Rapid analysis of data streams allows for quick, informed choices.

14. Continuous Improvement: Data-driven decisions often lead to a cycle of continuous improvement. As data is collected and analyzed, organizations can refine their strategies and tactics over time.

15. Monitoring Progress: Data helps track the progress and performance of various metrics and goals. It enables organizations to measure success and make mid-course corrections.

16. Compliance and Regulation: In regulated industries, organizations rely on data to ensure they comply with industry standards and regulations.

17. Ethical Considerations: Data can also be used to address ethical considerations. For instance, it can help identify and rectify biases in decision-making processes.

18. Data Visualization: Effective data visualization tools and techniques make complex data more understandable and enable decision-makers to interpret data with ease.

19. Data Governance: Implementing data governance practices is essential to ensure data accuracy, security, and accessibility. Well-managed data is crucial for making sound decisions.

20. Data-Driven Culture: Organizations that prioritize data-driven decision-making foster a culture of innovation and continuous learning.

In summary, data empowers decision-makers by providing them with actionable insights, enabling better risk management, fostering transparency, and promoting accountability. In today's data-driven world, the ability to collect, analyze, and leverage data effectively is a critical skill for individuals and organizations alike.

Key Metrics and Tools for Success

Key metrics and tools for success can vary depending on the specific context of your goals and objectives, whether you're measuring success in business, marketing, personal growth, or any other area. Here are some general key metrics and tools that are commonly used to measure and achieve success in various domains:

1. Business Metrics:

- **Revenue and Profit:** The fundamental metrics for business success. Tools like QuickBooks, Xero, and Excel are commonly used to track financial data.

- **Customer Acquisition Cost (CAC):** Measures how much it costs to acquire a new customer. Calculate by dividing your marketing and sales costs by the number of new customers.

- **Customer Lifetime Value (CLV):** Calculates the total revenue a business can expect from a single customer. Tools like Kissmetrics and Google Analytics can help with CLV analysis.

- **Conversion Rate:** Measures the percentage of website visitors who take a desired action, like making a purchase or signing up. Google Analytics and Optimizely can help track this metric.

2. Marketing Metrics:

- **Click-Through Rate (CTR):** Measures the effectiveness of your online ads and email campaigns. Google Ads and email marketing platforms provide CTR data.
- **Return on Investment (ROI):** Indicates the profitability of marketing campaigns. Tools like HubSpot and Marketo offer ROI tracking.
- **Customer Engagement:** Metrics like social media engagement, email open rates, and time spent on your website. Tools like Hootsuite, MailChimp, and Google Analytics can help.

3. Personal Growth Metrics:

- **Goal Achievement:** Track your progress toward personal goals using journals, goal-setting apps, or project management tools like Trello or Asana.
- **Mental Health:** Use mood-tracking apps like Daylio or journaling apps to monitor and improve your mental well-being.
- **Learning Progress:** Tools like Coursera, edX, and Duolingo can help track your progress in acquiring new skills and knowledge.

4. Fitness Metrics:

- **Steps Taken**: Use wearable fitness trackers or smartphone apps to measure daily steps and activity levels.
- **Calories Burned:** Fitness trackers like Fitbit or apps like MyFitnessPal can help monitor calorie expenditure.
- **Body Measurements:** Tools like FitTrack or Withings can track weight, body fat percentage, and other body measurements.

5. Project Management Metrics:
- **Task Completion**: Project management tools like Asana, Trello, and Jira can help track individual and team task completion.
- **Project Progress:** Tools like Gantt charts in Microsoft Project or online project management platforms like Monday.com help visualize project timelines.

6. Website and App Metrics:
- **User Engagement:** Google Analytics and Mixpanel can provide insights into user behavior, page views, and time spent on your website or app.
- **Conversion Funnel:** Track user flow and conversions through your website using tools like Google Analytics and Hotjar.

7. Customer Satisfaction Metrics:

- **Net Promoter Score (NPS):** Measure customer loyalty and satisfaction using NPS surveys.

- **Customer Feedback:** Tools like SurveyMonkey or Typeform can help collect and analyze customer feedback.

8. Social Media Metrics:

- **Follower Growth:** Track the growth of your social media audience using built-in analytics or third-party tools.

- **Engagement Metrics:** Monitor likes, shares, comments, and click-throughs using social media analytics tools or platform-specific insights.

These are just a few examples of key metrics and tools for success in different areas. The specific metrics and tools you need will depend on your goals and objectives. It's essential to define clear objectives and regularly measure progress to determine what's working and where improvements are needed.

Chapter 7

Influencer Partnerships

Influencer partnerships are collaborative relationships between individuals or organizations and influencers to leverage their reach, credibility, and expertise in promoting products, services, or causes. Influencer marketing has become a prominent strategy for businesses and brands looking to connect with their target audience more authentically and engagingly. Here are the key aspects of influencer partnerships:

1. Identifying the Right Influencers: - Select influencers whose content and audience align with your brand or campaign goals.

   - Consider factors like niche, follower demographics, engagement rates, and the influencer's authenticity.

2. Setting Clear Objectives: - Define specific goals for the partnership, whether it's to increase brand awareness, drive sales, or promote a particular message.

3. Negotiating Terms and Compensation: - Determine the terms of the partnership, including deliverables, duration, compensation, and the scope of work.

   - Compensation can include monetary payments, free products, affiliate commissions, or a combination of these.

4. Authenticity and Transparency: - Encourage influencers to maintain authenticity in their content and disclose sponsored content or partnerships by relevant advertising guidelines.

5. Creative Collaboration: - Work collaboratively with influencers on content creation. Share your brand's guidelines, but also allow them creative freedom to engage their audience effectively.

6. Content Sharing and Promotion: - Share the influencer's content on your channels to maximize reach. Cross-promotion can be a win-win strategy.

7. Monitoring and Analytics: - Use tracking tools and analytics to measure the success of the partnership. Evaluate key performance indicators (KPIs) related to your objectives.

8. Building Long-Term Relationships: - Consider forming long-term partnerships with influencers who genuinely align with your brand. These relationships can be more authentic and sustainable.

9. Compliance and Legal Considerations: - Ensure that influencer partnerships comply with advertising and disclosure regulations in your region. Legal counsel may be necessary.

10. Diversity and Inclusion: - Consider working with a diverse group of influencers to reach a broader audience.

11. Micro-Influencers and Nano-Influencers: - Don't overlook smaller influencers (micro-influencers and nano-influencers). They may have highly engaged, niche audiences.

12. Crisis Management: - Be prepared for potential issues, such as negative influencer behavior or backlash. Develop a crisis management plan.

13. Feedback and Improvement: - Seek feedback from influencers after a campaign to understand their perspective and make improvements for future partnerships.

14. Ethical Considerations: - Ensure that the influencers you partner with align with your brand's values and ethical standards.

15. Measuring ROI: - Calculate the return on investment to assess the effectiveness of influencer partnerships. Consider both quantitative and qualitative measures. Influencer partnerships can be a valuable strategy for businesses and organizations looking to expand their reach and engage with their target audience in a more personal and relatable manner. When executed well, these partnerships can lead to increased brand awareness, improved customer trust, and ultimately, positive business outcomes.

Collaborating with influencers

Collaborating with influencers can be a powerful way to promote your brand, product, or message to a targeted and engaged audience. Successful influencer collaborations require careful planning and a well-thought-out strategy. Here's a step-by-step guide on how to collaborate with influencers effectively:

1. Set Clear Objectives: - Determine your goals and what you aim to achieve through influencer collaboration. It could be increasing brand awareness, driving sales, or promoting a specific campaign.

2. Identify the Right Influencers: - Research and select influencers whose values, niche, and audience align with your brand or campaign. Consider factors like their follower demographics, engagement rates, and authenticity.

3. Develop a Creative Brief: - Create a detailed creative brief that outlines the campaign's objectives, key messages, guidelines, and any specific content requirements. This document will serve as a reference for the influencers.

4. Reach Out and Build Relationships: - Approach influencers with personalized, respectful messages. Explain your collaboration proposal, including compensation (if applicable), and how it benefits both parties. Building a positive relationship is essential.

5. Negotiate Terms and Compensation: - Discuss and agree upon the terms of the collaboration, including deliverables, compensation (whether monetary or in-kind), campaign duration, and exclusivity agreements.

6. Legal and Disclosure Compliance: - Ensure that the collaboration complies with relevant advertising and disclosure regulations in your region. Require influencers to disclose their partnership with your brand.

7. Collaborative Content Creation: - Work closely with the influencer to create content that resonates with their audience and aligns with your brand. Encourage their creativity while providing necessary guidance.

8. Content Approval Process: - Establish a process for reviewing and approving influencer-generated content before it's published. This ensures that it aligns with your brand's values and campaign objectives.

9. Promote the Content: - Once the content is live, actively share it on your own brand's channels. Cross-promotion can help maximize the campaign's reach.

10. Monitor and Measure Performance: - Use analytics and tracking tools to measure the success of the collaboration. Evaluate key performance indicators (KPIs) related to your campaign objectives.

11. Payment and Incentives: - Ensure timely and agreed-upon payments to influencers for their work. You may also consider offering additional incentives based on performance.

12. Build Long-Term Relationships: - Consider forming long-term partnerships with influencers who have a strong connection with your brand. Long-term collaborations can be more authentic and impactful.

13. Diversity and Inclusion: - Work with a diverse group of influencers to reach a broader audience. Promote inclusivity in your campaigns.

14. Ethical Considerations: - Ensure that the influencers you collaborate with align with your brand's values and ethical standards. It's important to maintain a positive and trustworthy image.

15. Feedback and Improvement: - Seek feedback from influencers after a campaign to understand their perspective and make improvements for future collaborations. Collaborating with influencers can be a valuable component of your marketing and promotional efforts. When done thoughtfully and with a genuine connection to your target audience, influencer collaborations can result in increased brand visibility, authentic engagement, and positive outcomes for your brand or cause.

Measuring the return on investment (ROI) of influencer marketing

Measuring the return on investment (ROI) of influencer marketing is crucial to assess the effectiveness of your campaigns and justify your marketing budget. Here's a step-by-step guide on how to measure influencer marketing ROI:

1. Set Clear Goals and KPIs: - Start by defining specific, measurable objectives for your influencer marketing campaigns. These goals could include increasing website traffic, generating sales, boosting brand awareness, or growing your social media following.

2. Track Campaign Costs: - Calculate the total cost of your influencer marketing campaign, including payments to influencers, product giveaways, content creation costs, and any associated fees (e.g., platform fees).

3. Monitor Reach and Engagement: - Use analytics tools to track the reach and engagement of your influencer's content. Metrics to consider include likes, comments, shares, views, and the number of followers gained during the campaign.

4. Measure Web Traffic and Conversions:- Track the increase in website traffic from referral links included in influencer posts. Use tools like

Google Analytics to monitor page views, click-through rates, and other website traffic data.

5. Implement UTM Parameters: - Use UTM parameters in the links shared by influencers to differentiate traffic sources. This allows you to attribute conversions directly to influencer marketing efforts.

6. Analyze Sales and Revenue:- Monitor the number of sales or conversions generated as a result of the influencer campaign. If possible, attribute specific revenue figures to these conversions.

7. Calculate Customer Acquisition Cost (CAC): - Determine how much it costs to acquire each customer through influencer marketing. Divide the total campaign cost by the number of customers acquired during the campaign.

8. Calculate ROI: - Calculate the ROI using the following formula:

ROI = (Net Profit - Campaign Cost) / Campaign Cost

 - Net Profit can be calculated by subtracting all campaign costs, including influencer fees and expenses, from the revenue generated.

9. Assess Non-Monetary Benefits: - Beyond financial gains, consider other benefits such as increased brand awareness, improved reputation, and engagement with a new or wider audience.

10. Compare to Benchmarks: - Compare your influencer marketing ROI to industry benchmarks or past campaigns. This provides context for evaluating performance.

11. Survey or Interviews: - Consider conducting surveys or interviews with customers to gather qualitative data about their awareness and perception of your brand due to influencer marketing.

12. A/B Testing: - Use A/B testing to compare influencer marketing efforts with other marketing channels to determine which provides the best ROI.

13. Long-Term Analysis: - Assess the long-term impact of influencer marketing on customer retention and lifetime value (CLV). Measure how influencer-generated customers perform over time.

14. Calculate Influencer-Specific Metrics: - Calculate influencer-specific metrics, such as cost per engagement, cost per click, or cost per follower gained. These metrics can help you assess the efficiency of individual influencers.

15. Continuous Improvement: - Use the insights from ROI measurements to fine-tune your influencer marketing strategy. Optimize your campaigns based on what works best for your brand.

Measuring influencer marketing ROI is an ongoing process. It's essential to refine your approach based on the data you collect and continuously adapt your strategies to achieve the best results. By following these steps and carefully tracking your campaign's performance, you can make data-driven decisions to enhance the effectiveness of your influencer marketing efforts.

Chapter 8

Paid Advertising and Budgeting

Paid advertising is a crucial component of many marketing strategies, helping businesses reach a wider audience, generate leads, and drive sales. Effective budgeting is essential for maximizing the ROI of your paid advertising campaigns. Here's a step-by-step guide on paid advertising and budgeting:

1. Define Your Advertising Goals: - Start by clearly defining your advertising objectives. Are you looking to increase website traffic, generate leads, boost sales, promote a new product, or raise brand awareness?

2. Identify Your Target Audience: - Determine your target audience based on demographics, interests, behaviors, and other relevant criteria. This audience will influence your choice of advertising platforms and budget allocation.

3. Select Advertising Platforms: - Choose the most suitable advertising platforms based on your target audience and goals. Common platforms include Google Ads, Facebook Ads, Instagram Ads, Twitter Ads, LinkedIn Ads, and more.

4. Conduct Keyword Research (For Paid Search Advertising): - If you're using paid search advertising (e.g., Google Ads), conduct keyword research to identify the most relevant and cost-effective keywords for your campaign.

5. Set a Budget: - Determine the budget for your paid advertising campaign. Consider factors like your overall marketing budget, campaign goals, competition, and the potential return on investment.

6. Allocate Budget Across Campaigns: - If you're running multiple advertising campaigns simultaneously, allocate your budget across campaigns based on their priority and expected outcomes.

7. Define Bidding Strategies (For Paid Search and Social Advertising): - Choose a bidding strategy that aligns with your objectives. Options may include manual bidding, automatic bidding, cost-per-click (CPC), cost-per-acquisition (CPA), or return on ad spend (ROAS) bidding.

8. Test and Optimize:- Start with a small portion of your budget to test your advertising campaigns. Monitor the performance, analyze results, and make adjustments as needed to improve effectiveness.

9. Measure Key Metrics: - Track key performance indicators (KPIs) such as click-through rate (CTR), conversion rate, cost per click (CPC), cost per acquisition (CPA), return on investment (ROI), and ad spend.

10. Scale Successful Campaigns: - If a campaign is performing well and delivering a positive ROI, consider increasing the budget to scale the campaign while maintaining performance.

11. Monitor and Adjust Regularly: - Continuously monitor your campaigns and make adjustments as necessary. This could include pausing underperforming ads, refining targeting, or modifying ad creatives.

12. Plan for Seasonal Campaigns: - Allocate the budget for seasonal or peak periods, as needed. Adjust your advertising strategy to accommodate increased competition during busy seasons.

13. Explore Retargeting and Remarketing: - Implement retargeting and remarketing campaigns to reach users who have previously engaged with your brand but didn't convert.

14. Budget for Ad Creative and Content: - Allocate a portion of your budget for creating compelling ad creatives, graphics, and ad copy that resonate with your target audience.

15. Test Ad Variations: - A/B tests different ad variations to identify which elements (headlines, images, call-to-action buttons, etc.) drive the best results. This iterative process can help you refine your ads.

16. Leverage Analytics and Conversion Tracking:- Implement analytics and conversion tracking to measure the impact of your paid advertising campaigns accurately.

17. Stay Informed and Adapt: - Stay updated with changes in advertising platforms and industry trends. Be prepared to adapt your strategy to stay competitive.

Effective paid advertising and budgeting require a strategic approach, ongoing monitoring, and the flexibility to adjust your campaigns based on performance. By setting clear objectives, allocating your budget wisely, and continuously optimizing your advertising efforts, you can achieve a strong return on investment and reach your marketing goals.

Effectively using paid social media ads

Effectively using paid social media ads can significantly boost your brand's visibility, engagement, and conversion rates. Here are some key strategies for making the most of your paid social media advertising campaigns:

1. Define Clear Objectives: - Start by setting specific and measurable goals for your social media ad campaigns. Common objectives include increasing website traffic, generating leads, boosting sales, or raising brand awareness.

2. Choose the Right Social Platforms: - Select the social media platforms that align with your target audience. Different platforms cater to various demographics and interests, so your choice should be based on where your audience spends the most time.

3. Understand Your Audience: - Create detailed audience personas to understand your target audience's demographics, interests, and behaviors. This information will guide your ad targeting.

4. Select Ad Formats: - Each social media platform offers a variety of ad formats, such as image ads, video ads, carousel ads, and story ads. Choose the format that best suits your campaign objectives and creative assets.

5. Set a Realistic Budget: - Allocate an appropriate budget for your paid social media campaigns. Consider your overall marketing budget, campaign goals, and the competitiveness of your target audience.

6. Refine Ad Targeting: - Use the platforms' targeting options to reach the most relevant audience. This can include factors like demographics, location, interests, behaviors, and retargeting.

7. A/B Test Ad Variations: - Test different ad creatives, headlines, and ad copy to determine what resonates best with your audience. A/B testing allows you to refine your ads for better performance.

8. Leverage Custom Audiences: - Utilize custom audience options to retarget users who have previously engaged with your brand, such as website visitors, email subscribers, or app users.

9. Implement Lookalike Audiences: - Create lookalike audiences based on your existing customer or user base. Social platforms can find new users who share characteristics with your current audience.

10. Use Ad Scheduling: - Schedule your ads to run during peak engagement times for your target audience. This can maximize the effectiveness of your campaigns.

11. Create Compelling Ad Content:- Design visually appealing and engaging ad creatives. The ad content should be relevant, informative, and persuasive. Ensure that your call to action is clear and compelling.

12. Monitor Ad Performance: - Continuously track the performance of your social media ads. Look at key metrics like click-through rates (CTR), conversion rates, ad spend, and return on ad spend (ROAS).

13. Optimize Ad Campaigns: - Based on performance data, make data-driven optimizations. This might include pausing underperforming ads, adjusting targeting, or increasing budgets for high-performing campaigns.

14. Implement Ad Landing Pages: - Direct users to dedicated landing pages that align with the ad's message and objective. Landing pages should be optimized for conversions and provide a seamless user experience.

15. Focus on Mobile Optimization:- Given the prevalence of mobile device usage, ensure that your ads and landing pages are mobile-friendly for a better user experience.

16. Be Adaptable: - Social media platforms are continually evolving. Stay informed about changes in algorithms, ad features, and industry trends, and adjust your strategies accordingly.

17. Use Analytics and Conversion Tracking: - Implement analytics and conversion tracking to measure the impact of your paid social media campaigns accurately.

18. Experiment with Video Content:- Video content tends to perform well on social media.

Experiment with different video formats, such as explainer videos, live streams, and short clips.

19. Stay Informed About Ad Policies: - Be aware of each platform's advertising policies to ensure compliance and avoid ad disapprovals.

20. Test Campaign Objectives: - Social platforms offer various campaign objectives, such as reach, engagement, traffic, conversions, and more. Test different objectives to see which best aligns with your goals.

Effective use of paid social media ads involves a strategic approach, consistent monitoring, and the flexibility to adjust your campaigns based on performance data. By following these strategies, you can maximize the impact of your social media advertising efforts and achieve your marketing goals.

Budgeting and cost optimization

Budgeting and cost optimization are critical aspects of financial management for individuals and businesses. Here's a comprehensive guide on how to effectively budget and optimize costs:

1. Set Clear Financial Goals: - Define your short-term and long-term financial goals, such as saving for a vacation, buying a home, or expanding your business. These goals will guide your budgeting and cost-optimization efforts.

2. Create a Budget:- Develop a detailed budget that outlines your income, expenses, and savings goals. Categorize your expenses as fixed (e.g., rent or mortgage) or variable (e.g., groceries, entertainment).

3. Track Your Spending: - Monitor your spending regularly to ensure it aligns with your budget. Use budgeting apps or spreadsheets to record transactions and analyze your financial habits.

4. Prioritize Saving: - Make saving a priority by allocating a portion of your income to savings, investments, or retirement accounts. Automate these contributions to ensure consistency.

5. Reduce Unnecessary Expenses: - Identify non-essential expenses and cut back on discretionary spending. This may include dining out less frequently, canceling unused subscriptions, or finding more cost-effective alternatives.

6. Negotiate Bills:- Contact service providers, such as internet or cable companies, to negotiate lower bills or explore available discounts.

Reducing fixed costs can significantly impact your budget.

7. Shop Smart: - Compare prices, use coupons, and take advantage of sales and discounts when making purchases. Consider buying generic or store-brand products to save on essentials.

8. Plan for Irregular Expenses: - Budget for irregular or annual expenses like insurance premiums, holiday gifts, or vehicle maintenance. Set aside funds regularly to cover these costs when they arise.

9. Build an Emergency Fund: - Create an emergency fund to cover unexpected expenses or financial setbacks. Aim to save three to six months' worth of living expenses.

10. Consolidate Debt: - If you have high-interest debts, consider consolidating them into lower-interest loans or credit cards. Reducing interest payments can free up more funds for saving and investment.

11. Optimize Tax Planning: - Maximize tax deductions and credits by keeping track of eligible expenses. Consult with a tax professional to explore potential savings opportunities.

12. Review and Adjust Your Budget: - Regularly review your budget to assess your progress and adjust it as needed. Life circumstances change, and your budget should adapt accordingly.

13. Consider Long-Term Investments: - Invest in assets that have the potential for long-term growth, such as stocks, bonds, real estate, or retirement accounts. Diversify your investments to manage risk.

14. Seek Professional Advice: - Consult with a financial advisor or accountant to gain insights into advanced financial planning and investment strategies.

15. Automate Saving and Investing: - Set up automatic transfers to savings and investment accounts on payday. This ensures that you consistently save and invest before spending.

16. Optimize Business Costs: - For businesses, analyze all expenses, including overhead, supply costs, and staffing. Look for areas where you can reduce costs without sacrificing quality.

17. Monitor Key Performance Indicators (KPIs): - In a business context, track KPIs related to profitability, customer acquisition cost, and customer lifetime value. Use data to identify areas for improvement.

18. **Leverage Technology:** - Use financial management apps and tools to streamline budgeting, expense tracking, and financial analysis. Automation can make cost optimization more efficient.

19. **Educate Yourself:** - Continuously educate yourself about personal finance, investment strategies, and cost optimization techniques. Stay informed about economic trends and market opportunities.

20. Stay Disciplined:- Consistency and discipline are key to effective budgeting and cost optimization. Stick to your financial plan even when faced with temptations or unexpected financial challenges.

Effective budgeting and cost optimization require discipline, regular monitoring, and a commitment to your financial goals. By following these strategies, you can manage your finances more efficiently, save for the future, and achieve greater financial security.

Chapter 9

Harnessing the Power of Virality

Harnessing the power of virality is a desirable goal for many individuals, businesses, and content creators. Virality refers to content or information spreading rapidly and extensively across the internet. While achieving virality is not entirely predictable, some strategies can increase the likelihood of your content going viral:

1. **Understand Your Audience**: - Start by knowing your target audience. What resonates with them? What kind of content are they likely to share with their network?

2. **Create Shareable Content:** - Develop content that is highly shareable and relatable. This can include informative, entertaining, emotional, or humorous content.

3. **Utilize Storytelling**: - Craft compelling stories that capture people's attention and emotions. Stories are more likely to be shared than straightforward information.

4. **Leverage Trends and Current Events:** - Stay up-to-date with trending topics and current events. Creating content that relates to or comments on these can boost your chances of going viral.

5. **Create Visual and Interactive Content:** - Visual content, such as images, infographics, and videos, tends to perform well. Interactive content, like quizzes or challenges, can also engage users.

6. Collaborate with Influencers: - Partner with influencers or individuals who have a substantial following. Their endorsement and sharing can increase your content's reach.

7. Timing Matters: - Be aware of the best times to post your content on social media. Peak activity times for your target audience can maximize visibility.

8. Encourage Sharing: - Include clear calls-to-action (CTAs) in your content to encourage sharing. Ask viewers to "like," "share," or "tag a friend."

9. Experiment and A/B Test: - Experiment with different types of content and headlines. A/B testing can help identify what resonates best with your audience.

10. Use Hashtags: - Appropriate and trending hashtags can make your content discoverable to a broader audience, especially on platforms like Twitter and Instagram.

11. Focus on Quality: - High-quality content is more likely to gain traction. Invest in good production values and ensure your content looks and sounds professional.

12. Evoke Emotions: - Content that evokes strong emotions, whether it's happiness, surprise, anger, or sadness, is more shareable.

13. Engage with Your Audience: - Respond to comments and engage with your audience. Building a community around your content can lead to more shares and engagement.

14. Be Authentic: - Authenticity is crucial. People are more likely to share content that they believe is genuine and honest.

15. Monitor Analytics: - Analyze the performance of your content. Track metrics like shares, likes, comments, and reach to understand what works best.

16. Think Beyond Social Media: - Virality is not limited to social media. Content can go viral through email, forums, and other online communities.

17. Patience and Persistence:- Virality is not always immediate. Some viral content takes time to gain traction. Be persistent in your efforts.

18. Legal and Ethical Considerations: - Ensure that your content complies with copyright and ethical standards. Avoid controversial content that may harm your brand.

19. Adapt to Feedback: - Listen to feedback from your audience and adjust your content accordingly. Adapting to user preferences can improve your chances of going viral.

20. Seek Professional Help: - If you're a business or content creator, consider working with professionals who specialize in marketing and viral content creation.

Remember that not every piece of content will go viral, and the definition of "viral" varies widely. What's most important is consistently creating content that aligns with your goals and resonates with your audience. Over time, your efforts may lead to content that goes viral, extending your reach and impact.

Understanding viral content

Understanding viral content is essential for individuals and businesses looking to create content that resonates with a broad online audience. While predicting virality is challenging, certain characteristics and patterns are often found in viral content. Here's a breakdown of what viral content is and some key factors that contribute to it:

What Is Viral Content?
Viral content is any piece of online content (e.g., articles, videos, images, memes, social media posts) that spreads rapidly and widely across the internet, often through social sharing, email, or other digital communication methods. This content gains massive exposure and engagement within a short period.

Key Factors Contributing to Viral Content:
1. **Emotionally Compelling:** - Viral content typically evokes strong emotions, such as joy, surprise, anger, or sadness. Content that triggers an emotional response is more likely to be shared.

2. **Relatability:** - Content that resonates with a wide audience or addresses universal themes tends to go viral. People share content that they can relate to or that reflects shared experiences.

3. **Entertainment Value:** - Viral content often entertains, amuses, or educates. Humor and entertainment are powerful drivers of virality.

4. Visual Appeal: - Content with strong visual elements, such as striking images or engaging videos, is more shareable. Visual appeal captures attention and encourages sharing.

5. Timeliness and Relevance: - Content related to current events, trending topics, or popular culture is more likely to go viral. Timeliness and relevance play a crucial role in capturing audience interest.

6. Surprise or Uniqueness: - Content that is unexpected, surprising, or unique tends to stand out. Viral content often challenges conventions and breaks the mold.

7. Human Interest: - Stories that focus on human experiences, personal journeys, or acts of kindness often go viral. People connect with content that showcases the human element.

8. Practical Value: - Content that provides practical tips, solutions, or insights can gain traction. People like sharing information that benefits others.

9. Short and Snappy: - Concise and easily digestible content is more shareable. People prefer content they can quickly consume and pass on.

10. Calls-to-Action: - Including clear calls-to-action (CTAs) in your content can encourage sharing. Ask viewers to "like," "share," or "tag a friend."

11. Controversy and Debate: - While risky, content that sparks debate or controversy can go viral. However, it's essential to tread carefully to avoid negative consequences.

12. Community Building: - Content that fosters a sense of community or belonging can gain momentum. People share content that aligns with their identity or values.

13. Platform Optimization: - Understanding the specific platform you're using is crucial. Content optimized for each platform's format, algorithms, and user behavior has a better chance of going viral.

14. Luck and Timing: - Sometimes, going viral is a matter of luck and perfect timing. A combination of factors, including influential shares or endorsements, can lead to virality.

15. Shareability: - Content that is easy to share and engage with (e.g., social sharing buttons, embed codes) is more likely to be spread by users.

16. User-Generated Content: - Encouraging user-generated content and participation can lead to viral campaigns. User involvement often amplifies reach.

Remember that not every piece of content will go viral, and the definition of "viral" can vary widely. Virality is not always the primary goal, as creating quality content that engages your target audience is also crucial. Analyze the characteristics of viral content, but focus on creating content that aligns with your objectives and resonates with your audience. Over time, your efforts may lead to content that goes viral and extends your reach and impact.

Viral marketing

Viral marketing is a powerful and cost-effective strategy for spreading your message or promoting your product to a broad audience. While there's no guaranteed formula for creating viral content, several strategies can increase the likelihood of your marketing campaign going viral. Here are some key strategies for viral marketing:

1. Create High-Quality Content: - The foundation of viral marketing is high-quality, engaging content. Content can take various forms, including articles, videos, infographics, memes, and more. Invest in creating content that is visually appealing, informative, and shareable.

2. Emotionally Engaging Content: - Content that elicits strong emotions is more likely to be shared. Emotional appeal can include humor, surprise, awe, inspiration, or empathy.

3. Tap into Trends and Pop Culture: - Stay up to date with current events, trends, and pop culture references. Create content that relates to these topics to tap into the existing buzz.

4. User-Generated Content: - Encourage your audience to create and share content related to your brand or product. User-generated content can be highly effective in spreading your message.

5. Leverage Social Proof: - Highlight endorsements, testimonials, and social proof in your content. People are more likely to share content that is backed by positive reviews and recommendations.

6. Contests and Challenges: - Launch contests or challenges that encourage participation and sharing. These can generate buzz and virality, especially on social media platforms.

7. Influencer Marketing: - Collaborate with influencers who have a substantial following in your niche. Influencers can help amplify your message and reach a broader audience.

8. Engage with the Audience: - Actively engage with your audience by responding to comments and starting conversations. A strong community can be a catalyst for virality.

9. Use Humor: - Humor is a powerful tool for creating viral content. People love to share funny videos, memes, and jokes.

10. Interactive Content: - Create interactive content, such as quizzes, polls, and interactive infographics. Interactive elements engage users and encourage sharing.

11. Surprising Twists: - Incorporate surprising or unexpected elements in your content. A twist or surprise ending can keep viewers engaged and sharing.

12. Storytelling: - Craft compelling and relatable stories that resonate with your target audience. Narratives are more shareable than straightforward marketing messages.

13. Timing Matters: - Be aware of when and where you release your content. Timing can significantly impact virality. Consider peak activity times on social media and relevant events.

14. Multi-Platform Strategy:
   - Share your content across multiple platforms and tailor it to each platform's format and audience. What works on one platform may not work on another.

15. Network Effect:- Leverage the network effect, where each share can lead to more shares. Encourage sharing by making it easy for users to share your content.

16. Use Visuals: - Visual content, such as images and videos, tends to perform well on social media. Invest in visually appealing and shareable content.

17. Teasers and Previews: - Create anticipation by releasing teasers or previews of your content before the official launch. This can build excitement and encourage sharing when the content is released.

18. Optimize for Mobile: - Ensure that your content is mobile-friendly. Many users access content on mobile devices, and mobile optimization is crucial for shareability.

19. Monitoring and Analysis: - Use analytics and tracking tools to measure the success of your viral marketing campaign. Analyze metrics like shares, likes, comments, reach, and engagement.

20. Learn from Viral Hits: - Study past viral content to understand what made it successful. Apply lessons learned to your future marketing efforts.

Remember that virality is not always predictable, and not every campaign will go viral. Focus on creating valuable content that resonates with your audience and aligns with your brand. Over time, your efforts may lead to content that goes viral and significantly increases your reach and impact.

Chapter 10

Secrets to Maintaining Relevance

Maintaining relevance in an ever-changing world, whether as an individual, business, or organization, is crucial for long-term success and growth. Here are some secrets to staying relevant:

1. Continuous Learning: - Stay curious and commit to lifelong learning. Keep up with industry trends, emerging technologies, and evolving best practices.

2. Adaptability: - Be flexible and open to change. Adapt to new circumstances, technologies, and customer preferences. Be willing to pivot when necessary.

3. Innovation: - Encourage a culture of innovation within your organization. Foster an environment where new ideas are welcomed and explored.

4. Customer-Centric Approach: - Put your customers or audience at the center of your decisions. Listen to their feedback and adapt your products or services to meet their changing needs.

5. Market Research: - Regularly conduct market research to understand your target audience and competitors. Stay informed about evolving customer preferences and behaviors.

6. Networking: - Build and maintain a strong network of industry peers, mentors, and collaborators. Networking can provide insights and opportunities for growth.

7. Embrace Technology: - Leverage technology to streamline processes, improve efficiency, and enhance customer experiences. Embrace digital transformation.

8. Content Marketing:- Stay engaged with your audience through content marketing. Share valuable and relevant content that addresses their needs and interests.

9. Personal Branding: - As an individual, cultivate a personal brand that showcases your expertise and passions. Consistently communicate your value and expertise to your network.

10. Diversify: - Diversify your skills, products, or services to remain relevant in a changing market. Explore new growth opportunities.

11. Stay Current: - Regularly update your skills and knowledge. Take courses, attend conferences, and participate in training to stay current in your field.

12. Customer Service: - Provide excellent customer service. A positive customer experience can lead to loyalty and word-of-mouth recommendations.

13. Data-Driven Decisions:- Use data analytics to make informed decisions. Data can reveal insights into customer behavior and market trends.

14. Anticipate Trends:- Try to anticipate future trends and changes in your industry. Being ahead of the curve can give you a competitive advantage.

15. Brand Authenticity: - Maintain brand authenticity. Authenticity fosters trust and helps you connect with your audience on a deeper level.

16. Competitive Analysis:- Keep a close eye on your competitors. Understand their strengths and weaknesses and use this information to position your brand effectively.

17. Sustainability and Social Responsibility: - Embrace sustainability and social responsibility. Modern consumers often support brands that align with their values.

18. Quality Control: - Ensure that your products or services consistently meet high-quality standards. Quality control is essential for long-term success.

19. Feedback Loop: - Establish a feedback loop with customers and employees. Use feedback to make improvements and innovations.

20. Mentorship and Coaching: - Seek mentorship and coaching to gain insights from experienced individuals. A mentor can provide guidance and perspective.

21. Resilience: - Be resilient and adaptable in the face of challenges. Resilience allows you to overcome setbacks and continue to grow.

22. Reevaluate and Reinvent: - Periodically reevaluate your strategies and business models. Don't be afraid to reinvent yourself or your business to meet changing needs.

Maintaining relevance is an ongoing process that requires a proactive approach, a willingness to evolve, and a commitment to delivering value to your audience or customers. By staying attuned to changes in your industry and continuously seeking opportunities for growth and improvement, you can remain relevant and thrive in a dynamic world.

Staying Updated with Trends

Staying updated with trends is essential for individuals, businesses, and organizations looking to remain relevant and make informed decisions. Here are some strategies to help you stay updated with current trends:

1. Set Up Alerts: - Use online tools and services to set up alerts for topics, keywords, or industries you want to monitor. Google Alerts and social media notifications are helpful for this purpose.

2. Follow Industry News Sources:- Subscribe to and regularly read industry-specific publications, magazines, blogs, and newsletters. These sources provide in-depth insights into trends and developments.

3. Social Media Monitoring:- Follow influencers, thought leaders and organizations related to your field on social media platforms. Social media is a valuable source of real-time updates and discussions.

4. Attend Conferences and Webinars: - Participate in industry conferences, webinars, and workshops. These events are opportunities to learn about the latest trends and network with professionals.

5. Join Professional Associations:- Consider joining professional associations or organizations related to your field. They often provide access to resources, research, and events.

6. Network and Collaborate: - Engage with peers, colleagues, and mentors within your industry. Collaborate on projects, share insights, and learn from one another.

7. Online Communities and Forums: - Participate in online forums and communities related to your industry. Websites like Reddit and Quora can be valuable sources of information.

8. Podcasts and Webcasts: - Listen to podcasts and watch webcasts that focus on trends and emerging topics in your field. Many industry experts host informative shows.

9. Read Books and Research Reports: - Explore books and research reports authored by experts in your industry. These sources often provide deep insights into emerging trends.

10. Analyze Competitors: - Monitor your competitors and their activities. Understanding what others in your field are doing can shed light on industry trends.

11. Subscribe to Trend Reports:- Subscribe to trend reports or market research services that provide regular updates on industry trends and consumer behavior.

12. Google Trends: - Use Google Trends to explore trending search topics and keywords related to your field. It's a valuable tool for understanding search trends.

13. Innovation Hubs and Incubators:- Explore innovation hubs, incubators, and startup communities. These hubs often lead to adopting and driving new trends.

14. Mentorship and Advisory Boards: - Seek mentorship from experienced professionals who can provide insights into emerging trends. Join advisory boards for fresh perspectives.

15. Diversify Your Interests: - Be open to exploring trends and topics outside your immediate field. Cross-disciplinary knowledge can spark innovation.

16. Experiment and Test: - Be willing to experiment with new approaches and technologies. Testing new strategies can give you firsthand experience with emerging trends.

17. Regularly Review and Reflect: - Schedule time for regular trend reviews and reflection. Evaluate how trends may impact your business or career and adjust your strategies accordingly.

18. Forecasting and Scenario Planning:- Engage in trend forecasting and scenario planning exercises to anticipate future developments and potential disruptions.

19. Continual Education: - Invest in courses and certifications that focus on emerging trends. Online learning platforms offer a wide range of options.

20. Feedback from Customers or Audience: - Pay attention to feedback from your customers or audience. They can provide insights into changing preferences and needs.

Staying updated with trends requires a proactive and multifaceted approach. By combining various strategies and regularly dedicating time to stay informed, you can adapt to changes in your industry, identify opportunities, and make informed decisions that keep you or your business relevant and competitive.

Adapting to Algorithm Changes

Adapting to algorithm changes, particularly on social media and search platforms, is essential to maintain your online visibility and engagement. Algorithms often evolve to improve user experiences, but these changes can impact content reach and performance. Here are some strategies for adapting to algorithm changes effectively:

1. Stay Informed: - Keep an eye on updates and announcements from the platform or service that has changed its algorithm. Understand the specifics of the update and its implications.

2. Analyze the Changes: - Examine how the algorithm changes affect your content's reach and engagement. Look at key metrics and assess the impact on your audience's interactions.

3. Diversify Content Types: - The algorithm might favor certain content types, such as videos, images, or long-form articles. Diversify your content to align with these preferences.

4. Quality over Quantity: - Algorithms increasingly prioritize content quality over quantity. Focus on creating valuable, relevant, and engaging content that resonates with your audience.

5. Engage with Your Audience: - Encourage user engagement through comments, likes, shares, and direct messages. The algorithm may favor content that generates interaction.

6. Utilize Live Video and Stories: - Live video and Stories are often promoted by algorithms due to their real-time and ephemeral nature. Incorporate them into your content strategy.

7. Optimize for Mobile: - Ensure your website and content are mobile-friendly. Many users access content from mobile devices, and mobile optimization can positively impact rankings.

8. Post Consistently: - Maintain a regular posting schedule to keep your audience engaged. Consistency signals to algorithms that your content is active and relevant.

9. Leverage Hashtags: - Use relevant and trending hashtags to increase the discoverability of your content. Research the most effective hashtags for your niche.

10. User-Generated Content:
   - Encourage your audience to create and share content related to your brand or products. User-

generated content often performs well under algorithms.

11. Consider Paid Promotion: - In response to algorithm changes, allocate a budget for paid advertising. This ensures that your content reaches a broader audience.

12. Engage with Trends: - Create content related to trending topics or hashtags, when relevant to your brand or niche. Staying current can help you leverage algorithmic changes.

13. Collaborate with Influencers: - Partner with influencers who have a substantial following. Their endorsement can help boost your content's visibility.

14. Long-Form and Evergreen Content:- Algorithms may favor long-form and evergreen content that provides value over time. Invest in in-depth articles, guides, and tutorials.

15. Track Performance: - Continuously monitor the performance of your content. Use analytics to identify trends and adjust your strategies accordingly.

16. Consider Multiple Platforms: - Diversify your online presence by using multiple platforms. If an algorithm change negatively impacts one platform, others can provide backup.

17. Seek Expert Advice: - Consult with experts or agencies experienced in adapting to algorithm changes, especially for platforms critical to your business or brand.

18. Community Building:- Build a loyal and engaged online community. Communities are less likely to be affected by algorithm changes because of their organic engagement.

19. Adapt and Evolve: - Be willing to adapt your strategies and approach as algorithms evolve. What worked yesterday might not work tomorrow.

20. Data-Driven Decision-Making: - Use data and performance metrics to make informed decisions about your content and strategies. Data-driven insights can guide your adaptations. Adapting to algorithm changes is an ongoing process. By staying informed, diversifying your content, and fostering engagement with your audience, you can navigate algorithmic shifts and continue to effectively reach and connect with your target audience.

Chapter 11

Measuring Success and ROI

Measuring success and return on investment (ROI) is crucial for evaluating the effectiveness of your efforts and making data-driven decisions. Whether you're an individual, a business, or an organization, understanding how to measure success and ROI is essential. Here are some key steps and strategies to help you do so effectively:

1. Define Clear Goals and Objectives: - Before you can measure success, you need to establish clear and specific goals. What do you want to achieve? Are you aiming to increase sales, grow your audience, or enhance brand awareness?

2. Identify Key Performance Indicators (KPIs):- Determine the KPIs that align with your goals. KPIs can vary depending on your specific objectives and may include metrics like revenue, website traffic, conversion rates, customer acquisition cost, customer lifetime value, social media engagement, or brand mentions.

3. Track and Analyze Data: - Use data analytics tools and software to monitor your performance and gather relevant data. Track KPIs consistently over time to identify trends and patterns.

4. Set Benchmarks: - Establish benchmarks or baseline measurements to compare your current performance against past results. This allows you to gauge progress.

5. Calculate ROI: - To calculate ROI, compare the financial gains (profits, revenue) generated from your efforts to the costs (marketing, advertising, labor, etc.) associated with those efforts. The formula is ROI = (Net Profit / Cost) x 100.

6. Attribution Modeling: - Understand how different channels and touchpoints contribute to your ROI. Attribution modeling helps allocate credit to various interactions in the customer journey.

7. Customer Feedback and Surveys: - Gather customer feedback and conduct surveys to gauge satisfaction and gather insights about their experiences with your products or services.

8. Qualitative Assessment: - Consider qualitative data, such as customer testimonials, reviews, and feedback, to understand the impact of your efforts on customer satisfaction and loyalty.

9. A/B Testing: - Conduct A/B tests to compare the performance of different strategies, campaigns, or variations of content. This helps you identify what resonates most with your audience.

10. Return on Ad Spend (ROAS): - For advertising campaigns, calculate ROAS by dividing the revenue generated by the cost of the advertising. ROAS = (Revenue from Ads / Cost of Ads).

11. Cost-Per-Acquisition (CPA): - Calculate the CPA by dividing the total cost of acquiring customers by the number of new customers acquired. CPA = (Cost / Number of New Customers).

12. Lifetime Value of Customers (LTV): - Determine the LTV by estimating the total revenue a customer is expected to generate during their engagement with your business. This helps you assess the long-term impact of your efforts.

13. Segmentation and Cohort Analysis: - Analyze your data by segmenting your audience or customers based on different criteria. Cohort analysis can provide insights into the behavior and performance of specific groups over time.

14. Marketing Attribution Models: - Employ marketing attribution models, such as first-touch, last-touch, or multi-touch attribution, to understand how various marketing channels contribute to conversions and ROI.

15. Regular Reporting: - Create regular reports that summarize your key metrics and findings. These reports can provide a clear picture of your success and areas for improvement.

16. Adjust Strategies: - Based on your measurements and analysis, make adjustments to your strategies and tactics. Eliminate or modify activities that do not contribute to your goals.

17. Communicate Results: - Share your results and findings with stakeholders, team members, or clients. Effective communication is essential for aligning everyone's understanding of success.

18. Continual Improvement: - Success measurement is an ongoing process. Continually refine your goals, KPIs, and strategies as your business or objectives evolve.

19. Seek Professional Assistance: - Consider consulting with experts or professionals who specialize in data analysis and ROI measurement if you need additional support.

20. Stay Informed: - Keep up to date with industry best practices and emerging measurement techniques. The digital landscape is continually evolving, and staying informed is essential for accurate measurement.

Measuring success and ROI requires a combination of quantitative and qualitative data, an understanding of your specific objectives, and a commitment to continuous improvement. By following these steps and leveraging the appropriate metrics and tools, you can effectively perform.

Defining Success Metrics

Defining success metrics is a crucial step in any project or initiative, as it allows you to measure progress and determine whether your efforts are achieving the desired outcomes. Success metrics are specific, quantifiable indicators that help you assess how well you are meeting your goals and objectives. Here's a step-by-step guide to help you define success metrics effectively: measure the impact of your efforts and make informed decisions to optimize your

1. Identify Your Goals and Objectives: Start by clearly defining the goals and objectives of your project or initiative. What do you want to achieve? Be as specific as possible and ensure that your goals are realistic and measurable.

2. Determine Key Performance Indicators (KPIs): KPIs are specific metrics that directly align with your goals and objectives. These are the indicators that will help you measure success. For example, if your goal is to increase website traffic, KPIs might include the number of unique visitors, page views, or time spent on the site.

3. Ensure Relevance: Make sure that your chosen KPIs are relevant to your goals. They should directly reflect the success factors that matter most to your project or initiative.

4. Set Targets: Define specific targets or benchmarks for each KPI. These targets should be achievable and time-bound, allowing you to track progress over a specified period.

5. Prioritize Metrics: While it's important to track various metrics, prioritize them based on their significance. Identify the primary and secondary metrics to focus your efforts and resources efficiently.

6. Align Metrics with Stakeholder Expectations: Ensure that your chosen metrics align with the expectations of key stakeholders, such as management, team members, and investors. This alignment helps in building consensus and support for your goals.

7. Consider Leading and Lagging Indicators: Leading indicators are predictive metrics that can indicate future performance while lagging indicators reflect past performance. Combining both can provide a more comprehensive view of progress.

8. Define Data Sources and Collection Methods: Determine where and how you will collect data for your chosen metrics. This may involve using analytics tools, surveys, customer feedback, or other data sources.

9. Create a Monitoring and Reporting Plan: Develop a plan for regularly monitoring and reporting on your metrics. This plan should outline who is responsible for collecting data, how often it will be reported, and how it will be communicated to stakeholders.

10. Review and Adjust: Periodically review your success metrics to ensure they remain relevant and align with changing goals or circumstances. Be prepared to adjust them as needed.

11. Communicate Progress: Regularly communicate progress and results to your team and stakeholders, and be transparent about whether you are meeting your targets. This helps keep everyone informed and engaged in achieving success.

12. Continuously Improve: Use the data and insights from your success metrics to make informed decisions and improvements in your project or initiative. Learning from your metrics is a key part of the process.

Remember that success metrics are not set in stone and may evolve as your project progresses. It's essential to be adaptable and responsive to changing circumstances and regularly revisit and refine your metrics to ensure they remain aligned with your goals.

Calculating Return on Investment

Calculating Return on Investment (ROI) is a fundamental financial metric used to assess the profitability and efficiency of an investment or project. ROI measures the gain or loss generated relative to the amount of money invested. To calculate ROI, use the following formula:

ROI = (Net Profit / Investment Cost) x 100

Where:

- Net Profit refers to the total return or gain generated from the investment, which is calculated as (Total Revenue - Total Costs).
- Investment Cost is the initial amount of money you invested in the project or asset.

Here's a step-by-step guide on how to calculate ROI:

1. Determine Net Profit: Calculate the total net profit generated by the investment. This involves subtracting all costs associated with the investment from the total revenue it generated. Be sure to include all expenses, such as operating costs, taxes, and any other relevant costs.

   Net Profit = Total Revenue - Total Costs

2. Identify the Investment Cost: The investment cost is the initial amount of money you invested in the project or asset. It may include the purchase price, acquisition costs, or any other expenses directly related to the investment.

3. Use the ROI Formula: Plug the values you've determined for net profit and investment cost into the ROI formula:

ROI = (Net Profit / Investment Cost) x 100

4. Convert to Percentage: Multiply the result by 100 to express ROI as a percentage. This step is necessary to present the ROI in a more easily understandable format.

5. Interpret the ROI: A positive ROI indicates that your investment is profitable. A higher ROI is generally better, as it represents a more substantial return relative to the investment cost. Conversely, a negative ROI suggests a loss.

It's important to note that ROI is a simple and powerful metric, but it has some limitations. It doesn't account for the time value of money (the idea that a dollar today is worth more than a dollar in the future) and doesn't consider the risk associated with the investment. Therefore, when interpreting ROI, it's essential to consider other factors, such as the investment's time horizon, risk, and opportunity cost.

Additionally, ROI can vary widely depending on the type of investment or project being evaluated.

For example, ROI for a financial investment like stocks is calculated differently than ROI for a real estate investment or marketing campaign. Always ensure that you use the appropriate inputs and considerations for the specific context of your investment analysis.

Chapter 12

Case Studies and Examples
Real-World Success Stories of social media marketer

Social media marketing has become a crucial component of digital marketing strategies for businesses and individuals alike. Here are a few real-world success stories of social media marketers or companies that have effectively leveraged social media platforms to achieve their goals:

1. Wendy's and Their Twitter Savvy: Wendy's, the fast-food chain, gained attention for its humorous presence on Twitter. Their tweets often playfully engage with customers and competitors. Their approach has not only increased their Twitter following but has also generated significant media coverage, making Wendy's a standout example of how a fun and engaging social media presence can boost brand recognition.

2. Nike and "Breaking2": Nike's "Breaking2" campaign used social media, primarily Twitter and Instagram, to promote their attempt to break the two-hour marathon barrier. The campaign generated a significant buzz and garnered global attention. Although they didn't achieve the sub-2-hour marathon time, the marketing success and brand exposure were significant.

3. Dove's "Real Beauty" Campaign: Dove's "Real Beauty" campaign challenged conventional beauty standards. They used social media platforms like Facebook and YouTube to share thought-provoking videos and content. The campaign resonated with a wide audience and went viral, reinforcing Dove's brand identity and message.

4. Oreo's Dunk in the Dark: Oreo's real-time marketing during the 2013 Super Bowl blackout is often cited as a textbook example of agile and responsive social media marketing. They quickly tweeted an image of an Oreo cookie with the caption, "You can still dunk in the dark," which received widespread attention and acclaim.

5. Airbnb's User-Generated Content: Airbnb has leveraged user-generated content on Instagram to showcase unique and beautiful properties listed on its platform. Their Instagram account features stunning photos from hosts and guests, which has not only driven engagement but also built trust among their user community.

6. Red Bull's Content Marketing: Red Bull is renowned for its content marketing strategy that focuses on extreme sports and adventure. They have used social media platforms like YouTube and Instagram to share visually captivating and adrenaline-pumping content that aligns with their brand image.

7. GoPro's User-Generated Content: GoPro encourages its customers to share their action-packed videos and photos captured with their cameras. They have successfully turned their customers into brand ambassadors through social media, creating a sense of community and excitement around their products.

These success stories emphasize the importance of creativity, engagement, and authenticity in social media marketing. Whether it's humor, thought-provoking content, real-time marketing, or user-generated content, each of these examples showcases how effective social media marketing can help businesses reach their target audience and achieve their marketing objectives.

Learning from Social Media Marketing Pioneers

Learning from social media marketing pioneers can provide valuable insights and inspiration for individuals and businesses looking to succeed in the digital marketing landscape. Here are some key lessons and strategies to glean from the pioneers of social media marketing:

1. Engagement and Authenticity:- Gary Vaynerchuk: Gary Vaynerchuk emphasizes the importance of authentic and meaningful engagement with your audience. He advocates for genuinely caring about your customers and providing value through content and interactions.

2. Content is King: - Seth Godin: Seth Godin is known for his emphasis on content marketing. He stresses the importance of creating remarkable content that stands out and resonates with your target audience.

3. Real-Time Marketing: - **Oreo:** Oreo's "Dunk in the Dark" tweet during the Super Bowl blackout demonstrated the power of real-time marketing. Being agile and responsive to current events can lead to viral moments.

4. User-Generated Content: - **Airbnb:** Airbnb's success comes in part from leveraging user-generated content to showcase the unique experiences offered by their hosts. Encouraging customers to share their stories can build trust and authenticity.

5. Storytelling: - **Coca-Cola**: Coca-Cola is a master of brand storytelling. They create emotional connections with their audience by telling compelling stories through social media. Their "Share a Coke" campaign is a great example.

6. Consistency and Frequency: - **Neil Patel**: Neil Patel, a renowned digital marketer, emphasizes the importance of consistent content creation and publishing. Regular, high-quality content can help build trust and brand authority.

7. Community Building: - **Red Bull:** Red Bull has created a community around its brand, especially in the extreme sports and adventure niche. Building a loyal and engaged community can lead to long-term success.

8. Data-Driven Decision-Making:- Avinash Kaushik: Avinash Kaushik is an analytics expert who highlights the importance of data in digital marketing. He encourages marketers to use data to make informed decisions, optimize campaigns, and understand user behavior.

9. Influencer Marketing:- Loreal and Influencers: Many beauty and fashion brands like L'Oréal have successfully partnered with influencers to promote their products. Influencer marketing can be highly effective when done right.

10. Experimentation and Innovation: - Snapchat: Snapchat revolutionized social media with its disappearing content format. The company's innovative approach showed that trying new ideas and formats can lead to industry disruption.

11. Cross-Platform Strategy: - Hootsuite: Hootsuite is a social media management platform that encourages brands to have a strong presence on multiple social media platforms. A diverse, cross-platform strategy can help reach a broader audience.

12. Adapt to Changing Algorithms:- Facebook and Instagram Marketing Experts: Adapting to the ever-changing algorithms on platforms like Facebook and Instagram is crucial. Staying up-to-date with best practices and algorithm changes is essential for success.

13. Sustainability and Responsibility: - **Patagonia**: Patagonia is known for its responsible and sustainability-driven approach to marketing. Authenticity in supporting social and environmental causes can resonate with consumers.

These pioneers and their success stories illustrate that there's no one-size-fits-all approach to social media marketing. Instead, it's about finding what works best for your brand, staying authentic, adapting to the ever-evolving digital landscape, and delivering value to your audience. Learning from their strategies and principles can help you navigate the dynamic world of social media marketing effectively.

Chapter 13

Conclusion

The Ongoing Evolution of Social Media Marketing
Social media marketing is a dynamic field that
continually evolves to adapt to changes in
technology, consumer behavior, and platform
algorithms. Here are some key aspects of the
ongoing evolution of social media marketing:

1. Platform Diversity: - New social media
platforms constantly emerge, each with its unique
features and audience. Marketers need to stay
informed about these platforms and assess which
ones are relevant to their target audience.

2. Video Dominance: - Video content, especially short-form videos and live streaming, has gained prominence. Platforms like TikTok, Instagram Reels, and YouTube Shorts have become essential for engaging with audiences.

3. Stories and Fleeting Content: - The rise of stories on platforms like Instagram, Facebook, and Snapchat has shifted how users consume content. Marketers need to create content that is engaging and fits the short-lived nature of these formats.

4. Ephemeral Messaging: - Messaging apps like WhatsApp, Facebook Messenger, and Instagram Direct have become popular for one-on-one communication. Brands are leveraging these platforms for personalized customer interactions.

5. User-Generated Content (UGC): - UGC continues to be a powerful tool. Brands encourage customers to create content related to their products or services, building trust and authenticity.

6. Influencer Marketing Maturation: - Influencer marketing has evolved from being a novelty to a structured and vital component of marketing strategies. Choosing the right influencers, measuring ROI, and maintaining authenticity are important.

7. AI and Chatbots:- Artificial intelligence and chatbots are used for automating customer service, personalizing user experiences, and data analysis to improve marketing strategies.

8. E-commerce Integration: - Social media platforms are integrating e-commerce features, such as shoppable posts and in-app checkout. This trend simplifies the customer journey from discovery to purchase.

9. Augmented Reality (AR) and Virtual Reality (VR): - AR filters and VR experiences are being integrated into social media marketing, offering immersive and interactive brand engagement.

10. Data Privacy and Regulation: - Increased concerns about data privacy and regulations like GDPR and CCPA are changing how marketers collect and use data. Marketers must adapt to more stringent rules and transparency requirements.

11. Sustainability and Social Responsibility:- Brands are expected to take a stance on social and environmental issues. Consumers are more likely to engage with and support companies that align with their values.

12. Content Quality and Authenticity: - Quality content that provides real value to the audience is becoming increasingly important. Authenticity and transparency are key elements for building trust.

13. Algorithm Changes: - Social media algorithms are continually updated, affecting organic reach. Marketers must stay agile and adapt strategies to reach their audience effectively.

14. Micro-Moments: - Marketers need to capture users' attention during "micro-moments" when they turn to their devices for quick answers or information. These moments are often localized and time-sensitive.

15. Data Analytics and Attribution: - Measuring the effectiveness of social media campaigns has become more sophisticated. Marketers rely on data analytics and attribution models to understand the customer journey and optimize their strategies.

The ongoing evolution of social media marketing underscores the need for marketers to stay informed, adaptable, and creative. Embracing new technologies, understanding changing consumer behaviors, and focusing on building genuine connections with audiences is key to success in this dynamic field.

Unleashing the Secrets for Lasting Success
Achieving lasting success in any area of life, whether it's in your personal or professional endeavors, often involves a combination of strategies and principles. While there is no one-size-fits-all formula, here are some key secrets to help you on your journey toward lasting success:

1. Clear Vision and Goals: - Define a clear vision of what success means to you. Set specific, achievable goals that align with this vision. Having a sense of purpose and direction is crucial.

2. Resilience and Perseverance: - Success rarely comes without setbacks and challenges. Resilience and the ability to persist in the face of adversity are essential qualities.

3. Continuous Learning: - Never stop learning and growing. Stay curious and open to new ideas. Acquiring new skills and knowledge can lead to ongoing success.

4. Adaptability and Flexibility: - The world is constantly changing, and the ability to adapt and be flexible in your approach is vital. Embrace change and be willing to pivot when necessary.

5. Hard Work and Discipline: - There's no substitute for hard work and discipline. Consistently putting in the effort and maintaining self-discipline are key to lasting success.

6. Time Management:- Efficiently manage your time by setting priorities and focusing on what matters most. Avoid distractions and time-wasting activities.

7. Building Strong Relationships: - Success is often a result of collaboration and networking. Cultivate positive relationships with mentors, peers, and your community.

8. Mental Resilience: - Cultivate mental resilience and a positive mindset. Your attitude and ability to bounce back from failures can be a determining factor in long-term success.

9. Embracing Failure:- Don't fear failure. View it as a learning opportunity. Some of the most successful people have experienced numerous failures on their path to success.

10. Financial Management:- Be responsible with your finances. Save and invest wisely, and avoid unnecessary debt. Financial stability is an important aspect of lasting success.

11. Self-Care: - Taking care of your physical and mental well-being is essential. Prioritize sleep, exercise, and relaxation to maintain good health.

12. Consistency and Habit Formation: - Consistent action leads to long-term results. Establish positive habits that support your goals and success.

13. Empathy and Emotional Intelligence:- Develop empathy and emotional intelligence to build better relationships and understand the needs and motivations of others.

14. Innovation and Creativity: - Encourage innovation and creative thinking in your endeavors. These qualities can set you apart and lead to lasting success.

15. Legacy and Impact:- Consider the legacy you want to leave behind and how your success can have a positive impact on others and society.

16. Purpose-Driven Success: - Align your success with a higher purpose or a cause you are passionate about. Success with a meaningful purpose is more likely to be lasting.

Remember that lasting success is not just about reaching a specific milestone but maintaining it over time. It's a journey that requires ongoing effort, adaptability, and a commitment to personal growth. There will be ups and downs, but by incorporating these secrets into your life, you can increase your chances of achieving and sustaining success in the long run.

Appreciation

Dear Readers,

As we conclude this journey through the "Major Secrets of Social Media Marketing," I want to express my deepest gratitude to each one of you. Thank you for investing your time and attention in exploring the dynamic world of social media strategies and unlocking the major secrets that drive success in the digital realm.

This book wouldn't have been possible without the support of my readers and the vibrant community that surrounds the ever-evolving landscape of social media. Your curiosity and commitment to staying ahead in the world of marketing inspire me, and I hope the insights shared within these pages have empowered you on your path to social media mastery.

Remember, the true magic lies not just in the secrets unveiled but in the application of knowledge. As you implement these strategies, adapt them to your unique brand, and navigate the ever-changing social media landscape, may you find continued success and fulfillment.

Thank you once again for being part of this journey. Wishing you abundant success in all your social media endeavors!

With heartfelt gratitude,

Moses Alfred

www.ingramcontent.com/pod-product-compliance
Lightning Source LLC
Chambersburg PA
CBHW072217290526
45794CB00004B/1782